Some of My Life Lessons

Joshua L. Holm

STANDING TRANSFORMING ENCOURAGING ENLIGHTENING LOVING

WWW.THEMANOFSTEEL.COM

For more info or additional copies contact below:
Soft cover 978-0-9863737-3-2
PUBLISHED BY S.T.E.P
(Steel, Training, Educational,Programs)
WWW.THEMANOFSTEEL.COM
Attn: S.T.E.E.L
PO BOX 550
Mineral Wells, TX 76068
Printed in the United States of America

Table of Contents

Some of My Life Lessons

About the Author:

JOSHUA L. HOLM was born and raised in Arkansas. There he met and married his high school sweet heart Crystal as he refers to as his Queen and Jewel. They moved to Killeen, Texas after Joshua switched from the reserves to active duty Military. He deployed to Iraq in 2003-2004 while in combat he was injured multiple times and put on crutches, and leg braces after returning home from his tour. In 2007 Joshua had a grand mal seizure and found out then that he had been living with Traumatic Brain Injury since 2003. In 2009 Joshua had another seizure and hit his head on the counter and the doctors found a cerebral hemorrhage. Joshua had lost feeling on the left side of his body and was in a wheel chair for the third time for almost two years. Joshua wrote his first book "Some of My Life Lessons" while in the wheel chair and had it published in December 2010. He realized that because of the realness of his injuries that he allowed them to cripple and crush all of his life goals, dreams, and aspirations. Joshua began to reflect on his past, and realized that he had turned many stumbling blocks into stepping stones. This gave him a passion that helped define his purpose. Joshua is the father of two wonderful children Rebecca and Ethan. The main turning point in his life was January 16, 2003 when he gave his life back to the Lord. Joshua now lives in Fort Worth, Texas with his wife and two children. This is what fuels him to teach others how to overcome challenges, and make their life count. Joshua & Crystal love to show others how they too can have freedom in all aspects of life despite all circumstances.

Joshua L. Holm is the founder of Steel Hope a non-profit organization that is dedicated to helping others. Steel Hope has a mission to build, equip, and empower others to be people who will continually BE STEEL! Believe Expand, Stand, Transform, Encourage, Enlighten, and Love around the world. By granting scholarships to go through other programs or eventually going through their programs, their goal is to restore hope and touch lives one person at a time. With your generous contributions they will be able to bring hope to many lives. Steel Hope has a heart to help but they can't do it without your help! Right now they are in the process of granting scholarships for people to attended needed training, educational, or rehabilitation programs to bring hope back into our communities' one person at a time. They have a vision to start a recreational facility where people will be able to attend financial classes and a fitness center where all can feel free. They also would like to have a place for people with disabilities to come and enjoy themselves and feel free. Building this takes money to buy land and build a facility Joshua has a vision for 1% of Americans to at least give $1 one time to show that despite all the hard times America Still stands strong and we will be a Pillar of Strength and Beacon of Hope for all to see that there is STEEL HOPE!

STEEL
H PE

"Our Heart Beats for Others"

Chapter 1: Growing Pains

It all began November, 1983 when I was born in Pocahontas, Arkansas to Lawrence and Judy Holm. I was their third child. Their first child, Christina Marie Holm, was a stillbirth. Jacob was their second and then came little old me, Joshua Lee Holm. I was raised in a good Christian home where good morals and manners were literally instilled in me. I simply chose a life of rebellion and, boy, did I choose it. My father and mother would tell me one thing and I would do the complete opposite of whatever they would say. You could say that I was a problem child…more like a little demon from Hell. There were many times when I was good but the bad outweighed the good. Since I had blonde hair and was not the best kid, many people called me Dennis the Menace. We have all heard of the terrible twos…I had the terrible threes. Before I was four years-old, I had already been to the hospital way too many times. I was a very hard-headed child that did not learn from his mistakes. This is just one of the reasons I am writing this book.

It all began when I listened to my older brother Jacob. He told me I could fly, so I stood in the sink and jumped from the sink into the bath tub. At that moment, I really thought

I could fly like Superman. I leapt from the sink and fell into the bath tub hitting my head which gashed open about an inch away from my left temple. When I stood up I was covered in blood from the gash which dripped down the front part of my body. The sight of me scared my brother so much that he took off in a dead run towards the back door. If it was not for my dad catching him on the way out, he would have run straight through the back glass door. Luckily, one of our next door neighbors was a nurse and she helped to slow the bleeding until I could be taken to the hospital. I was given a few stitches and was good as new, at least until the next time. It wasn't long until I did it again. No…not the Superman stunt but something entirely new.

With me there was no telling what I would do. Back then I seemed to know no boundaries. For some reason I thought putting a rock up my nose would be cool. It was, until it got stuck. You know how things are fun until you get hurt or until you lose. The fact of the matter is, when you can't fix things on your own, you have to ask for help. As a child, you really don't want to ask for help, especially from your mother or father. In kindergarten, I knew the principal's office inside and out. I probably spent more time in there than in my kindergarten class. It was never my fault, though. At the time, I believed it was everyone else's fault. I would always be minding my own business. Okay, who am I kidding? I blamed everyone else even though ninety percent of the time it truly was my fault. It was much easier and less painful to blame others rather than deal with the real issues.

One time I was playing on the playground and a boy hit me in the back of the head with a brick. Can you believe that little punk hit me on the head with a brick? What could he have been thinking? The truth is he probably wasn't thinking; that is the reason anybody would do such a thing. He probably did not even think of the harm it could have done if it hit the right spot. Turns out I wasn't thinking either because I turned around and grabbed the closest thing to me which just happened to be a lunch box. This was not just any lunch box, but an old-school metal princess lunch box. I smacked that kid in the head with it a few times. By the time I finished smacking him, it wasn't a lunch box anymore. Because I didn't think about what I was doing I made a very bad decision. I not only had to pay for that poor girl's lunch box, which happened to be a limited edition tin lunch box, but I also had to go to the office and get corporal punishment (also known as "getting my butt whooped"). As it turns out, I actually got into more trouble than the punk kid that started the fight.

The Bible says, "He who angers you controls you." Boy was this is a lesson I wished I had grasped a long time ago. Instead, I was such a class clown; I would crack jokes and pull pranks on some of my teachers and other students just to get a laugh out of everyone. My fourth grade teacher got so upset with me and my smart mouth that she literally tied me up with a jump rope. She tied my arms and legs to the desk so I could not move. She even tried to put duct tape on my mouth but was never able to do so. As unbelievable as this whole scene may seem, my mom actually caught her doing this. Boy was my mom mad at her. I have never in my life seen my mom that mad; I thought she was going to kill that teacher. She told me to sit outside the class room. I did not even argue with her because I knew my mom meant business. To this day, I do not know how my mom was able to control herself, because I would have probably hit anybody who did something like that to either one of my children. I am still learning self-control in some areas. My mom did the best thing that she could have done.

As I mentioned earlier, I was the class clown. Even though I knew how to do something, I would ask for help just to look stupid so others would laugh at me. You could say I was not very smart back then. My parents tried so hard to get me to behave, but I was unable to maintain good behavior for any extended period of time. It seemed every time I would try to change, someone or something would give me another reason not to do so. I always had a smart remark for any question someone may have had. I would seek out any opportunity to make people laugh. I enjoyed making people happy. I would often put myself down before anyone else had a chance to. Some people would call me a know-it-all; my response was that I was a know-some-of-it-all. I read the dictionary on a regular basis to increase my vocabulary. While this was a good habit, I would act stupid simply because I thought it gave me an advantage. I did not want to be considered a nerd; as it stood, I already wore glasses and did not want to give anybody anymore reason to call me one. For some reason I had it in my head that if people knew I was smart, they would expect more from me. In some ways this was true, but I took it completely out of context. I lived to regret this as my grades never reflected the knowledge that I had. My advice is this: if you are smart, act like it. Please do not try to be someone you are not. In the end you are still you and you are special just the way you are. There is no need to change for anyone other than God as you are perfected by His glory.

My father took me to church; he did not smoke, drink or curse. He was twenty-seven when he got his first kiss. It was to my mother on their wedding day. I did not fully realize how great that was until later on in life. I had never cherished the fact that there was purity in this type of relationship. I always saw my dad and mom as old farts. No offense, but I always saw them as boring and unable to relate to anything I was going through. How could they? I always felt they could never understand what it was like to be me. I later learned this was not always the case. I always thought my father and mother were trying to control me. I had no idea at the time that what they were trying to do was protect me from the hurts, disappointments and deceptions that this world has to offer. I remember when my father would spank me he would always say, "Son, this is going to hurt me more than it hurts you." I would think, "Yeah, right. You are not the one getting your butt whooped." I now realize he was right because the soreness of a spanking would eventually go away but the hurt that I gave him cut him deeper than any knife could ever cut him. I have found myself saying to my children the very same words that my father once told me. They look at me with that same look I once gave my dad. It is funny because as a child I never thought my parents could ever relate to what I was going through. Now that I have children of my own, I realize how wrong I was.

When we are children we can be very selfish. It is easy to shift the blame on our parents, our city, our environment or our racial upbringing for why we are the way we are. I wonder how many of us have stopped to think of the pain we have put our parents, our family, our spouse or even our friends through because of our selfish nature. Do we ever care? I know that I did not care how hurtful the words I spoke to my parents were. Sometimes, we seem to care about no one but ourselves. I know I was that way; it was all about me. I did not care how I got attention as long as I got it. I would do things that would get me in trouble just to be noticed by my parents. For some odd reason I would try to get in trouble at school just to get attention. As I got a little older my rebellious nature changed to something more than just attention-seeking. It became the fuel that I would live by for longer than I had ever dared to imagine.

One of my father's employees took advantage of me. I was in denial about it until another hurt child went to the police about the matter. I was hurt very badly. How could someone do something like this? How could I have been so deceived and so used? I felt dirty and nasty; I used to hug everyone I would meet. I used to sing at nursing homes and hug everybody there. I used to be so caring towards others. It changed me so that I did not want to be touched or even talked to. I was like a turtle that wanted to crawl back in its shell and hide. The fact is a part of me did die. I told my father and mother that nothing really happened. The reality was that it did happen, but I was so ashamed that I denied the fact of what really happened. I wished it was all a dream but it was not; I was not yet willing to face it. I allowed this violation to destroy my life.

It all started very innocently with a shrug of a shoulder here and there. I would tell my father and mother that I did not want to talk about it. I would sneak out of the house. I would hang out with people I did not even like just to prove a point. I was like a storm that was beginning to form. Before I knew it, I was a tornado destroying anything and anyone in my path. I realize all of this now, but back then, I did not care what I did to anyone. I would pick fights in school for no reason. Something in me was broken and it needed to be fixed. I was like a hurt dog biting the same hands that were trying to feed me and mend my wounds.

By the time I was twelve years-old, I was already drinking, smoking and cursing, amongst other bad behavior. I hid all kinds of secrets from my parents; I am sure they did not even know I was doing these things back then. They sure did not buy anything for or support the lifestyle I was living. I began to hate my life, my family, God, everyone and everything in the whole wide world. I thought my so-called friends were my family and would always be there. They were there when I would steal my dad's medicine so we could get high or when I took my mom's wedding band because they told me to. They were there when I had money, drugs or other things they wanted, but when I really needed them the most, they were nowhere to be found. I had already lost people close to me to drugs and different types of ungodly things. I joined a small wannabe gang which was actually worse than a real gang because they have no reputation to speak of. This forced us to prove ourselves in order to be cool and accepted. I was so immature and did a lot of stupid things I have now learned to regret. It got so bad that by the time I was thirteen my father and mother were ready to move to another city just to make things better for me. Would this help me or make matters even worse? How could I have allowed things in life to bring me down so low?

Chapter 2: Moving On

I was thirteen when my family and I moved to a smaller city with less people and less crime; it had to be better, right? It was a new start for all of us. I failed to realize that it was not the city or the people, but me that was the source of the real problem. I was too blind to see it back then; I now know pride had a lot to do with it as well. I started at a school that no soccer or track team. "This school sucks," I thought to myself. They did, however, have a choir and I have always loved to sing, so I joined the choir and J.R.O.T.C. (Junior Reserve Officers Training Corps).

The very first day of school I got detention for smiling at a teacher I argued with the detention teacher about how stupid it was to get detention for smiling, so they gave me corporal punishment. I was so mad I could have exploded. I got moved to this stupid little hick town, lost my so-called friends and now this happens? I began to wonder what else could possibly go wrong. They often say, "You can take a dog out of the pound but you cannot take the pound out of a dog." As the next few months went by, I began to find new so-called friends that smoke, drank and did other not so great things. Then I found myself egging houses, rolling houses and lots of other terrible things. I saw myself as a good person. Boy, was I deceived.

There were some people that I was nice to. I had a really good friend that really cared about me and his family accepted me as their own. His name was Johnathan Tucker but everyone always knew him as J.T. He had cerebral palsy and turned out to be a great friend. His mom, Ida, would always ask me how I was doing and mean it with an open heart. His dad, Dennis, was just as nice. They were able to give me good sound advice and tried to help me live a clean life. I remember taking a few trips with them. It was actually fun, but it didn't last. I turned back to the world for answers and got more hurt than I was before. I tried not to ever hurt them though I know through my faults I disappointed them. I never realized how much I hurt my father and mother. Now that it has happened, it is too late, but I am truly sorry for all the hurt and shame I put upon my true friends and family throughout the years.

Back to the story…by the time I was fourteen I was already suicidal. I really thought that there was nothing in the world to live for. I was very deceived, depressed and began popping my father's pain pills to try and ease the pain. It never worked. I tried screaming until I lost my voice. I tried everything I could think of but nothing could possibly fill the hole in my heart. I decided I was going to truly end it all. I had a knife in my hand and was preparing to slice my wrist. I remember saying, "No one loves me. No one cares about me." Just as I was going to slice my wrist, I heard a voice of an angel say, "Someone does love you and care about you." I wondered to myself if this was an angel that God sent to me. Throughout the years I have realized it was an angel…my angel. The angel was now my wife Crystal.

The same night I was down and almost out, God sent her

to me to save my life. I know that now but I did not realize it back then. I thought she was talking about herself, not the God that was living in her. A few years down the road, she started taking me to church with her. She was trying to help me live for God the way she was living for Him. We all know the old saying, "You can lead a horse to water but you can't make it drink." Boy was this true. Crystal and I started dating when I was still fourteen. My old ways began to pull her down with me. It was not long after that we started fornicating. She began to smoke a little with me, drink, and do all types of unreal things with me. Crystal's mom, Anita, warned her of her own mistakes and told her not to make the same ones she did. By the time I was a senior in high school I was already going to be a father.

I stopped doing some of the bad things I was doing. In an effort to move on, I joined the U.S. Army after turning seventeen. I was beginning to mature and was scared and excited all at the same time. I was going to be a father and I was totally unprepared. I had a choice to make to either man up or face reality or run from my commitments and be a dead beat dad. I decided to grow up and grow up fast. I worked two jobs and refereed soccer games on the weekends to provide for my soon-to-be family. I asked Crystal to marry me. I was shocked that she actually said yes. Crystal and I wed on May 18, 2002, the day after I graduated high school. In the few years before we tied the knot, I began to change. I stopped smoking and I gave up a lot of bad and illegal addictions. I still held on to some for a gloomy day. I joined the Army and went to basic training in between my sophomore and junior year of high school. We moved to Killeen, Texas, in late 2002. I was trying to be a good husband and father, or at least the best I knew how to be. I was providing for them financially but my life was going nowhere. How could I be moving on but not moving forward? I had no traction; I needed a true change. I realized that there was a lot of mental baggage holding me down and I could not move forward until I let go of it all. What are you holding on to today? Will you let it go?

Chapter 3: Letting Go

What is there to let go of, I thought to myself? What could possibly be holding me back? I was a soldier in the most powerful military force in the world. I had not even been married a year and yet I was already on the verge of a divorce. It was October 2002 and my wife and I were at a pawn shop when someone overheard me playing a keyboard. It was some old church song I remembered when I was a kid. They invited us to church. When I heard the word "church," it was like hearing nails on a chalk board. I thought to myself, Heck no!

The following Saturday someone from the same church was at our door trying to give us another invitation to the church. I remember I had a beer in my hand and tried to shut the door on them but my wife Crystal stayed and talked to them. We did not even do the normal concert scene Saturday night. Sunday came and my wife told me she is going to church. I said, "Have fun, baby." She replied with, "Ok, that is fine. You can watch Rebecca." I thought to myself, "You punk. I know you did not just tell me if I don't go with you, I have to watch our daughter!" I ended up going to church. Two weeks and two services later in the middle of the night, I was sawing some good logs and drooling like a dog all over my pillow.

Crystal wakes me up and says, "Pray with me so I don't go the Hell." I said a prayer with her just to shut her up but she meant it from her heart. As the next couple of months went by, I began to see changes in her life, some big and some small. I saw her begin to let things go and start to grow in Christ. It was like she was becoming a totally new person because she stopped arguing with me over stupid little things. She began to sing all the time and became very emotional and tender-hearted. I know most women are this way but she seemed to be a lot more emotional than usual. I thought to myself, "Where is my wife because this is not like her at all?"

I would try to argue with her by putting her down and telling her all kinds of other cruel and selfish things out of my ignorance; I did not understand why she did not even try to retaliate. She would simply tell me that she loved me and was praying for me to get saved. That would tick me off even more than if she had just yelled back at me. I would get upset and curse at her and put her down. She would cry and tell me that I was destroying our marriage.

I was an artillery soldier and would often be in the field training for battle. I never expected to be sent overseas. It was in November 2002 when my unit got orders to go to Iraq. We were on lockdown for a couple of weeks. I began to wonder how my wife could have changed so much. I was raised in church but there was just something about her transformation that I could not grasp…something new and crisp. It was January 2003 when I finally asked my wife, "What is it that you have that I don't have?" Her answer pierced my heart, "You have religion and I've got Jesus." Those words began to break down the pride that I had held on to for so long. It started to fade away in the same way the sun melts ice. I was speechless so I walked away.

I still tried to play it tough, but the truth is those words began to torment me. I began to think of how fake my whole walk with God was. I looked nice and did not have any tattoos or body piercings. Still, the truth was I looked alive and well but I was dead inside. I was much like an apple that is red and delicious until you take a closer look and see a small hole. By the time you bite it, it tastes bitter and disgusting. That was me: bitter and disgusting. I would take almost everything that was said to me out of proportion. I knew that I was broken and the Lord knows I could not have been trusted. The next night I could not eat, sleep or do anything without hearing those words pressing on me. I tried to act hard but for some reason I just could not move on. It hurt too much. For once in my life, I was faced with the truth; I was not used to someone calling me out like she had. For once in my life I had to make a decision that would affect everything in my life. I had no idea what I was going to do. It was like being pulled in half with part of me wanting and needing a change. The other part of me enjoyed my old life and did not want to change anything. This part of me wanted to run again. Almost all my life was spent running from situations that would cause me to slow down or put weight on me. This meant I ran from all types of commitments and always had an excuse to get out of any situation no matter how hard it may have seemed. I was a good talker and was told I could sell a chicken to an egg. This was the only time in my life I finally had no more excuses. I had to do something. I could either run again or get it right. On January 16, 2003, I rededicated my life to Jesus Christ. I finally let go of all my pride not knowing what would happen next.

Chapter 4: The Breaking Point

Everything in life has a breaking point whether it is as hard as a diamond or soft as a tissue. I tried to hold on to all the hurt, shame, guilt anger, and frustration because I did not want to get hurt again. I wished we could heal inside like we can on the outside with a process that lasts only a few days or a week at most. The truth is it can take years for us to heal on the inside. We must be willing to lay it all down and humble ourselves so God can have control.

Imagine playing a video game for the first time but knowing that beside us sits the game master, the one who wrote the game. He is the one who knows every single bit of the game. He knows every pitfall, trap and dead end. You have a choice to play the game with only one life to spare or to hand the controller to him? What would you do: try it on your own or let him have control? What I did for many years was to try it all on my own. I would see a dead end and turn around only to find another dead end. It was like I was in quick sand; the more I tried to resist the faster and further I would sink. The more I did things without God the worse things would get.

I tried alcohol, drugs, sex, money and church; nothing could fill the emptiness that I had in my life. When I drank, it felt really good at first, but at the end of the day, I was in the toilet throwing up all the good time I had just had. It never tasted as good coming up as it did going down. I tried drugs…a little marijuana here and there, acid, LSD and PCP, amongst others. It left me high but there was still no change and I always ended up broke. I tried living for money; it is good to have money, but if that is all you think about, it will wither away. At one point, I was making lots of money and had nothing to show for it. I was more worried about money than my family, including my daughter. I was like Scrooge McDuck from the show Duck Tails…too busy watching my money that I never had any time to enjoy it. I tried sex. I lost my virginity before I was fifteen. It felt good but it was not what I was looking for. I know now that at the time it was lust, not love. It still was not making me change. I tried going to church. I sang in the choir and at nursing homes and did good deeds for the elderly. Yet I still felt unchanged. What else could there possibly be? This is the question I asked myself over and over again and yet if someone were to ask me, I would lie to their face and tell them I was not looking for change.

Why does life have to be so hard? Why does this only happen to me? What is there to live for? No one loves me. I hate this world, my life and my family. You may have asked yourself these same questions or had these same thoughts yourself. I did until I decided I had had enough of this miserable life. I knew there had to be more out there than this. I was trying to change but I could not do it on my own. Something had me held down and at times it felt like I was being choked by something. I felt heavy and burdened as if I had weights tied to my feet. It seemed every time I would take a step forward, I would take three steps backwards. I was a good person most of the time. I was not a hard person to get along with. The truth was I was being choked by something; my flesh was choking my spirit. I had no idea the damage it was doing to me and those around me. It was like a poison that seeped into every little nick and crevice, killing everything it touched. I was heavy because the weights of the world were on me: depression, anger, malice, lust, lies and other deceptions of the world. I was bound by the chains of sin and there seemed to be no way out.

Every lock has a key. Some are big and some are small, but for every lock there is a way out. Whether you want to admit it or not, you have done some wrong things in your life. It may have been a little white lie that we often say in the hopes of being nice. It may have been stealing that one little piece of bubblegum, or cheating on a test, or changing the F on your report card to an A. No matter how little or big it is, it is still a sin. Sin is the lock that holds us from moving on; we are bound by it. The good news is there is a key. It is not good deeds, position or even how much you go to church. Yes, I am telling you church will not set us free from the bounds of sin and hell.

The key is Jesus Christ. He died on the cross to set us all free from the bounds of sin and Hell. Then why does everyone not accept Him? The truth is everyone, no matter how old they are, no matter what their race is, regardless of whether they are male or female, married or single has to come to a point in their life where they are sick and tired of being sick and tired. They will not be able to take another step or another breath without needing a change. Some people will feel there is not a need for change in their lives. Yet most of us are often hurt by people we love and care about the most including friends, family, schoolmates and even other church members. You better believe even people in church have the potential to burn you. Having tough skin is sometimes not even enough. The main problem is that most people have tried church but few have really experienced a true relationship with Jesus Christ. I told myself I would never go to church again but when I saw the change in my wife, I began to desire for it as well. I was able to stop fighting, let go and empty all the hurt and shame. As I confessed my sins to Jesus Christ I felt a change like I have never felt before. I was free…or was I? Even though I prayed a sinner's prayer, I did not feel completely free. How could this be?

I had to not only confess my sins to God but also walk away from them. This was the hardest part: knowing that you are free and letting go of every weight. This means whether you have been raped, lied to, abused physically or mentally, cheated on or abandoned, you have to let it all go before you can move forward or be free from all the pain. You have to forgive every one of all wrongdoings and realize it was not them but the sin living inside of them that betrayed you. Our sin is what put Jesus Christ on the cross. Every time we sin we become the Roman soldier with the whip in our hand ripping the skin off His back. Every time we sin we are driving the nails through Jesus' hands and feet.

My change did not happen overnight; I tried to hold on to something for a rainy day. I was on the fence. I wanted to change but something inside of me wanted the sin. It is easy to justify your actions but you cannot fool God. I realized that if I did not let go of all of it, I could never become the man God had called me to be. One day I tried to drink a beer and I had no desire for it anymore. I tried to curse and it seemed silly and stupid. What happened to me that I could see things so differently now? It was almost like I had a new set of eyes. God took the veils off of my eyelids so I could now see how my sin was affecting my life. It was my breaking point.

Remember, everything and everyone has a breaking point. No matter how bad or good a person you are, you will be broken either by this world or by God. The choice is yours, so choose wisely. The word of God says, "Every knee shall bow and every tongue will confess that Jesus Christ is Lord." Let it be before God comes back. Break your pride and let Jesus into your heart. Unlike most doors, your heart only has one handle and you must open it so God can come in and begin to change you. No matter how hard God tries or how many times he knocks at your heart's door, it cannot be opened unless you open it first. Then we can all be broken from the grasp of Hell.

Chapter 5: Born to Die

It seems like just yesterday I had the awesome privilege of watching my son Ethan being born into this world. I remember my wife lying on the table in labor for thirty-two hours and finding out she was going to have another c-section. I was there watching as the doctor delivered my son. I expected to see this beautiful boy come out...was I fooled. I remember the doctor reaching in and pulling out this baby that had all types of gooey looking stuff on it. I thought to myself, "What is that?" I smiled because I would never have said that out loud. In reality, I was waiting for someone to come in and snatch the baby to take it back to Area 51. I thought I was watching an alien movie where the people turn into aliens. They told me it was the after birth and all I could think was yuck! They asked me if I wanted to hold him. I said, "No, not like that!" Then the nurse cleaned him up; he was my boy.

I mention this to show that this is how everyone is born; none of us come out with a curl or a perm, or Mary Kay make-up on. We were born naked and in the goo. We have a residue that is on us that has to be washed off so we can be clean. Even though we look clean, are we really? If you wash only the outside of a cup, would you still drink from it? Why not? It has the residue of the old drink in it because we only cleaned the outside. It might look clean but if you take a drink, you will clearly see it is not. I know from experience; once I took a coffee cup out of the dishwasher, poured a glass of soda into it and drank. Instantly I thought, yuck! I poured all the soda out. The soda was clean but the cup was not. If you don't believe me take a yellow highlighter, write on your hand and then put your hand under a black light; it will glow. Now wash your hand with soap and water and the yellow will go away... or does it? Now put your hand under the black light again; even though the color is unseen by the human eye it still has a residue. This is true of everyone; we are all born in a residue called sin regardless of how clean we may look to others. God is like the black light; He can see what we as humans cannot. He can see the residue of sin.

Since the beginning of time when the first sin was committed, the residue of sin has been passed down from generation to generation. Sin is not biased. It is in every person no matter how good or bad that person is. Yes, Mother Theresa, the President of the United States, T.D. Jakes and Joel Osteen (I call him Happy Jack) were all born in sin. There are so many that are truly good people and they may think that is good enough. But when it is all said and done, no one is good but God. The truth is the day you are born is the day you begin to die. Let me explain what I mean here: as children we are very tender-hearted and are, for the most part, loving, generous, kind and trustworthy. As we grow we begin to experience life. We may become distant from others, cold-hearted, selfish, and ungrateful and so on. So right here we can see there are some things that are not always positive about growing up in this world. We begin to die to the characteristics that God placed divinely in every one of us. Even those like Saddam Hussein,

Hitler, Al Capone and Timothy McVeigh held it even though they did not tap into it.

The word of God says, "We have all sinned and fallen short of the glory of God." And, yes, that includes Oprah Winfrey. If we are born in sin, then how can we die to sin? We all have to be born again as new creatures and new creations. When we are born in the world we are all blind to the reality of life in the spiritual aspect. We can only see the outside of things but inside we are all dead. This is why we live to die. If we never die we are never really ever living but shall remain dead. It is almost like a car running with a bad alternator; once you kill the car engine the battery is dead because all the life is drained from it. I finally died to my flesh and became alive in my spirit.

My life has never been so good. I can see things in a whole new way. I can see things that I was once blind to. My life now has meaning to it because I have a purpose. We all do, but will we die to ourselves to be reborn in the spirit? Before a tree a can produce any fruit something in it must die so it can expand and reach out. It is easy to see how many seeds are in an apple but we often forget that it is impossible for us to see the amount of apples that are in one seed. When we are living only in the flesh we can never produce any good fruit because every seed we plant is toxic and is capable only of producing bad fruit. When we are born again as Christians then we can produce good fruit that will multiply and make more impact than we could ever see or imagine. Let us all die so we can live forever.

Chapter 6: No Turning Back

I remember when I was on the farm with my grandfather he would always let me and my brother Jacob ride on the tractors with him. He was a farmer who plowed the fields and I remember him telling me that you have to always look forward to keep the plow straight. I watched him plow so many times that I thought plowing was going to be a piece of cake. There are several times in our lives we look at something and think we can do this better than anyone else. I thought that just by keeping the plow straight it would be enough. I had no idea the reality of how hard it was to plow a field. It seemed easy but I always caught myself looking back to see how the plow was cutting into the dirt. I finally got the privilege of driving the tractor myself. I was so excited. It was my time to show these country boys that a city boy could do everything they could even though I was only able to visit a couple weeks out of the summer. They farmed for a living and they made fun of me because I was from the city and, thus, different. I was going to show them that I could farm better than they could. I got in the tractor, put my seat belt on, adjusted the seat and even checked the mirrors before I started to plow. As I began to plow, everything was going great until I forgot my

Grandfather's advice: "Don't ever look back." I looked back, and when I did, I messed up the whole field and it had to be plowed again.

The reason I mention this story is because very often in life we are so focused on what is left behind that we can never move forward. I was so focused on what was behind me I did not see that I was off course. How many of us often look back to see what we have left behind? You cannot focus on God and the world at the same time. I remember another time when I was kayaking with my father-in-law Greg. While we were on the water he told me to keep my eyes forward and to not look back or I would fall off balance. As we were kayaking, I began to think how easy it was and started looking all around watching everyone else instead of looking forward. I went down a waterfall. This particular waterfall is called Wall Slammer. You can imagine why. Since I was not focused, I was supposed to maneuver in mid-air to keep from hitting the wall. Needless to say, I hit the wall and, boy, did it hurt. It felt like I was hit by a car.

Why couldn't I have just stayed focused? Why did I take that fall? I looked back and fell hard; so often we think that what we leave behind is better than what we have now. I've heard it said that the grass is only greener on the other side because it is closer to the sewage. This is so true; I was bound by alcohol, big time, and other bad habits. I am now free of it all. Is it worth giving up my peace, love and joy that God instilled in me for that old filth? Not in a million years. Often people do it every day. Some people give up marriages after twenty plus years to have a new fling or feel younger. Give me a break; you're still old. Nothing against anyone, but I want to keep it real. The only way you will ever be loved or feel love is through Jesus Christ.

The Bible says that God is love. So this world is the total opposite of God. This world is full of bitterness, hatred, malice, backbiting, gossipers and other negativities that could have me going on for many pages. We all know how each and every one of us can think in ways of revenge due to the little mishaps in life. If you focus on the things in the past you will never be able to focus on the future or even the present. For many years I was focused on the pain that I felt inside and I could not move because I felt trapped. Every time I would begin to look ahead and try to focus on Godly things I would be reminded of my past life. I was blind to the fact that this was condemnation. The Bible says that Jesus did not come to condemn the world but that through Him the world might be saved.

I heard a sermon that was about there being no condemnation through Christ Jesus. I really thought about all the things that were going through my head and I begin to cry. How could I have been so deceived? I started burning the bridges to my past. I started with all the things I did that hurt people through my rebellious state of life. Then I thought about the curses I put on myself by getting involved in witchcraft. Then I moved on to the curses of fornicating and having my first child out of wedlock. As I began to let everything go one at a time, I was able to focus on God and walk forward without having all the guilt and shame of my sin. I began to realize every sin I committed was covered by the blood of Jesus Christ. I finally understood that Jesus died on the cross to set us all free of all the mistakes, guilt and shame of our sin. The Bible says, "No one having put their hand to the plough, and looking back is fit for the kingdom of God." Let us look ahead at what God is doing through our lives. We all must walk by faith and not by sight. We need to have faith that God is really there and is keeping us in His will.

It is easy to focus on the things around us and the trials we are facing. If we focus on God we will not be brought down by the fiery darts of Hell. We need to be focused on what is ahead because if not, we will be hit by every lie and deception of Hell. If we look ahead to the things to come we will not carry the extra weight of past failures and mishaps of our lives. Now that we are looking forward, we have to equip ourselves with the armor of God. Before you can ever fight, you first must be able to stand. Then next you must be able to plant your feet so firmly that when the attacks come, you can take them and still stand. Now, it is time to prepare for the battles to come.

The Bible says that a double-minded person is unstable in all of their ways. This is true because the best way to defeat any enemy is through confusion. If you cannot focus, you have no power. The devil loves confusion because it causes us to be unstable, and, thus easier to topple. Every time we fall it gets harder and harder to brush ourselves off and stand again. The Bible says that the devil is the author of confusion, and he will do anything to make us fall away from God's will for our lives. The Bible says that God is the author and finisher of our faith. We must never look back but always looking toward God in every trial, tribulation or test of faith. We will always be able to resist the devil and all his wicked ways, but first we must submit ourselves to God. This will cause the devil to flee from us all. Remember to always look ahead to the great things yet to come.

Chapter 7: A Better You

I remember the nineteen years that I lived for the world. I had no hope, true joy, peace or love for anyone or anything. I wasted nineteen years of my life living in sin and regretting my mistakes in life. Now I can turn the page and thank God for His wonderful grace and mercy. I have been sanctified and washed by blood and I am now free of all iniquity and unrighteousness. The amazing thing about God is that His records and files on us are not like a credit report. In the world, there is no room for redemption. I remember getting a credit card when I had my own maintenance company after getting out of the Army. I had some cash saved up but decided to use the credit card instead of my cash to start the business. Somehow the money I had saved got spent. It is not good to live like royalty when you are self-employed because the pay fluctuates from day to day. Some things happened where I had to let the business go due to my health. The credit card company wanted all of their money now. I honestly did not have it all because I had to pay employees and my bills as well. They did not want to hear my reasons; they wanted it paid in full or else they were going to add extra fees onto my current bill. I tried to pay as much as I could, but they kept adding extra fees here and there, raising the interest and other outrageous stuff. Finally, I let it hit my credit and, boy, did it hit it.

I learned from the experience, it but it hurt me. Thank God He is not like that Credit Card Company; He is a great and wonderful redeemer that builds and edifies His people. He does not kick us while we are down and He never calls us out. God erases all of our sins when we say a sinner's prayer. Unlike a credit report, God does not hold us down because of a couple of mistakes. He takes our mistakes and instead of burying us in the ground with them, He uses them to build us to be a wonderful testimony for His glory. Do not misunderstand my story. Credit is good, but if you make a mistake you have to prove yourself worthy and sometimes even that is not enough to fix past errors. There are a lot of times in our lives when we learn from our mistakes but are still reminded of them on a daily basis.

Today I had a big fight with my wife whom I love very much. You see, all I wanted for Father's Day was for my wife and kids to treat me; it did not matter if I got a steak or a dollar cheeseburger. I just wanted a gift from the heart. I don't know how to tell them how much they mean to me. I would do anything for my kids and my wife as well. My wife Crystal took what I said wrong, and we started arguing which then made my daughter Rebecca start to cry. Rebecca is very emotional at this age. She is starting to grow up. She is seven and is starting to take things very seriously. My wife dropped me off at HEB, our local grocery store, and I went in to get something to eat. I came out empty-handed because what I wanted could not be found in there. I wanted something from the heart that said I love, cherish and appreciate you. When we got home we all went inside and my four year-old son Ethan comes up to me and says, "Daddy, can I take you out?" I said,

"Yes, son, you can." He replied, "Where do you want to go?" I said, "I do not care, son." He then came back and said, "Is McDonald's fine?" I told him that was fine and then began to cry because that is all I wanted: a gift from the heart. So my wife took my son to McDonalds to get me a cheeseburger.

If this reminds you of yourself, do not hold back what is really inside of you. Just let it out. No one can read what you keep inside. This is a lesson that we all should learn from. As we grow in God, we can see so much more wrong in us and in the world. Just when you feel like you have figured it all out, another page turns and there are many new lessons in life you have never experienced. I remember watching a movie about these people who had a briefcase with instructions in it on how to fix the main power source. This boy knows there has to be a way out but everyone is telling him there is nothing out there. He gets a hold of the briefcase that gives step-by-step instructions on how to get out of this world. The world is beginning to fall apart a little at a time. The instruction manual has keys that lead him into the right direction. At the end of the movie, the boy and another girl find the way out. Everyone told them that there was nothing but darkness outside of their world. They finally get out and see nothing but darkness. They start to look back at what they were leaving to be in this new world. Then the sun begins to rise and they are astonished at this new world. No more wondering if the power source is going to go out. This is how we are when we are lost in the world; we begin to think that there has to be more to our life than just this. I was so much like this boy; deep down in my heart I knew there had to be more to life than this.

I was searching around looking for answers to all the problems I was going through. First I tried looking for everything in the world. This made me feel deader inside than

I felt before. It almost felt like it was sucking the little life I had left out of me. Then, I finally found an instruction book that gave me directions. It gave me a clear and specific path to follow that would bring me to the light. I knew by following this path I would be free of all the pain and misery I was going through at the time. Do you need a change? Are you tired of knowing there has to be more to life than this?

There is a manual that can give you all the answers to any question you may have. The manual is the Holy Bible. This is the answer to any trial or test of faith you are going through. I remember when I was in the military, I worked in intelligence and we had all types of secure networks and programs that were encoded. They had to be decoded before they could be read and understood. These programs needed a key to be able to decipher them. The Bible or the word of God has to be decoded before it can be understood. If there is no key, it looks like gibberish and has no meaning. Jesus Christ is the key to unlocking all the secrets that the word of God has to offer.

Before you can receive the key that unlocks doors of unlimited knowledge, wisdom and a clear direction, you must first follow a few steps. It is as simple as ABC. First, you must admit you are a sinner and that you are in need of a savior. This means realizing that you have not been a good boss of your own life. You need someone to take charge and give you direction. Second, believe in your heart that Jesus Christ lived a sinless life and traded His life for our sins; believe that He died on the cross to set us free of all guilt, shame and pain that the world has given us due to the sin of the world. Third, confess with your mouth that Jesus is the Lord of your life; open the door to your heart that only you can open to allow Him in to change your life. No one can open the door to your heart but you. Not this world, not the devil, not religion and

Not even Jesus Christ Himself can do this for you. This is a decision that only you can make.

The ABC's of salvation are Accepting, Believing, Confessing so if you do these three things, you will open a whole new dimension of living. I have been truly saved and delivered since January 16, 2003. It was the best decision I have ever made in my life. It has not always been easy being a Christian, which entails being Christ-like and walking in His footsteps. Often we think that being a good person or doing good deeds is enough. The Bible says that faith without works is dead. This means that having faith alone is not enough. We must put this faith in action because, if we do not, it will be dead. It is much like going to the store and buying a plant but never preparing the ground or planting it so it can fortify the roots that it has. This is something you must do daily. Not bi-weekly, not once a month or once a year, but daily. Never look back. Everyone and everything behind you is dead and gone. Look forward to life and live more abundantly with Christ Jesus.

Chapter 8: You are not alone

I remember being a young boy. I would lie in my bed and hear the thunder and lightning. I would start to shake and so badly did I want to run to my mom and dad's door and ask them, "I am scared so can I sleep with you?"Though I never did; instead I stayed balled up in the covers shaking in fear. I was also afraid of going to the toilet because, when I was little my brother Jacob told me about the toilet monster.

I was afraid it was going to bite my butt or pull me down into the toilet. As silly as these things seem now, they were true fears back then.

I remember my mom test-driving a new car and driving to the store to buy something. My older brother Jacob put me in the trunk; he told me it would be fun and that he would pay me to stay in there for a minute. I counted for a minute and said, "Ok, now let me out." There was no response. At first I thought he could not hear me so I hollered even louder... still no response. I started to kick the trunk thinking he might be outside and away from the car where he could not hear me. Then it hit me. I was all alone and in total darkness. How could I have been so deceived? I trusted him and never thought he would do this to me. I began to panic thinking I was going to die in the trunk of this car. I was so scared that

I peed all over the trunk. Finally, he opened the trunk and I saw the light; the fear went away. I began to get mad because he tricked me. Then, he showed me a pull strap that opens the trunk just in case someone locks you in it. So the whole time I was panicking and thinking I was going to die, there was a way out. I just could not see it because I was so busy focusing on the darkness that I could not see the way of escape right in front of me. This was the key to set me free and out of the darkness.

I tell this story because this is exactly how the devil plays us. He will first deceive you by telling you to step out of the light and into the darkness. By putting you in total darkness, he gains control; you are helpless and feel trapped. The whole time he is controlling you, he makes you believe there is no way out. We are so busy focusing on the darkness around us that we do not see the key that would set us free from the darkness. We begin to panic and fear that we are dead and that there is no way out. He makes us believe that God cannot hear us calling out for help. He knows that as long as we think we are alone, he will have the control. See, he will do anything he can to see us stray from God's will for our lives. He will tell you any lie because he knows that his days are numbered. He does not want to spend eternity in Hell alone. He wants to take anyone he can with him. The Bible says that he roars around like a lion seeking whom he may devour. Will it be you?

I was so scared because I had no control and I could not even see my hand in front of my face. I felt as if I could not breathe and my heart began to beat like a drum. I thought I was going to die in there. I began to sweat because it was so hot in there. I thought to myself, can anyone hear me? Am I all alone? From that, I learned not to trust. I remember watching the movie "Home Alone" and I would laugh my head off because the thieves were so stupid and predictable. Much like the main character, Kevin, in the movie, I would always try to make traps to catch whoever might try to bring harm to me. As I began to grow up, I realized that there are no monsters in the toilet, in the closet or even under the bed. It is all in our minds. But there is a real enemy.

We can really come up with some crazy things in our minds. When we are left alone, our thought process can get really weird. Some people talk to themselves, pretend they are something or someone else, plot out murder scenes in their minds or think of how to harm someone who did them wrong. I know I did all these and more. I would have fantasies of all types of sin. These were not only physical sins but spiritual ones as well. The real enemy is the devil. The worst thing he can do is to make us believe that he does not exist. How can you fear something you cannot see? We, as Christians and followers of Christ, and Americana as a whole, have been conditioned. We are like frogs in water. If you turn the heat up quickly, a frog will realize the water is getting hot and jump out. Yet, if you turn the heat up slowly, the frog will never notice the change and will eventually succumb to the heat. We as a Christian nation should see the change and warn others of this before it is too late. So why don't we? Are we too busy with the distractions of the world to care? Are our lives centered on only ourselves? Is it our jobs, our money or our families?

I really saw the change when I went to the Dr Pepper museum in Waco, Texas. I was watching a video of commercials and saw how the world changed dramatically between the 1960s and 2000s. I saw how people began to show a little more skin or say sexual innuendos. These things were around before but they were not seen by everyone. Only to those who had their

SOME OF MY LIFE LESSONS

eyes on and in the world did the devil have fooled. He had me fooled for many years, until my eyes were opened to see the truth. Over the past few years I have seen just a glimpse of the damage that was done because of my sin. I realized that we are never really alone because God is always there. See, God has always been there since the beginning of time; however, because of our sin there is a bridge that separates us from Him. Until we decide to burn that bridge that allows Him access to us, we will feel alone.

Have you ever felt scared? It is not a pleasant feeling, is it? Have you ever felt like you were all alone? So many times in our lives we seem to run scared not knowing who to trust and who not to trust. First, let me start by telling you that you are not alone. The Bible says that God will never leave you nor forsake you. So why do we often choose to leave the one that is there to help us? Why do we leave God? What are we selling ourselves out for? What will you sell your salvation out for and at what price? See, the devil will do anything he can to ensure you do not live for God. The devil loves division, discord and separation of saints. When we are alone, we are very vulnerable to the lies of Hell. The Bible says, "Whoever angers you controls you." Who is controlling you? When are you in charge? What are you a slave to?

For many years I was being controlled by the world. I was blind to this fact for a very long time. We often seem to forget that we are very weak without God there to make us strong. The Bible says, "Through our weaknesses, God is made strong." What needs to be weakened in your life so God can be in control? Is it your pride? Is it a love for material things? There is nothing wrong with wealth or possessions as long as they do not make you stray from God or His will for your life. Why can't we hunger for God the way we hunger for food? Why can't we thirst for God and His Holy Spirit the way a plant thirsts for the morning dew? Why can't we wait on God like the moon waits for the sun to go down before emerges? The truth is we can, but we often choose not to. So my question for you is what are you hungry for? What do you thirst for? What are you waiting on?

The Bible says, "Keep asking, and it will be given to you. Keep searching and you will find. Keep knocking and the door will be opened for you." Will you answer the door when God is knocking? These are my life lessons. I am so thankful for God and His grace and mercy. When I was lost, blind, and bound by sin, Jesus was still there for me. When I turned my back on Him, he was still there waiting patiently for me to call Him back into my life. The Bible says that "God is married to the backslider." If this is you, open your eyes and see the true light of Jesus Christ. The Bible says that Jesus is the way, the truth and the life. No one can come to God but through His son Jesus. We are not promised tomorrow, so make a change now before it is too late.

I would never be the man I am today without my wonderful, beautiful wife Crystal. Throughout the years, she has been the crown that has kept my mind on God and His will for my life. She has been there to tell me when I stink and need to take a shower, both spiritually and physically. She has fortified me and believed in me even though I didn't always believe in myself. These are my life lessons so far. Keep your eyes on Jesus Christ and you will never go wrong. I hope you all have learned a little or at least have been reminded of what we are here for. Let this book be a tool that God can use to help you learn and share with others through your own life lessons. This is the first of many books that God has shown me to write. Please look forward to more books in the near future. This is my seed of hope and I want nothing more than to it to be seen and shared all over the world. It is up to us all to do our part to "Keep the Fire Burning"!

Made in the USA
Columbia, SC
29 June 2022